NO LONGER PROPERTY OF
ANYTHINK LIBRARIES/
RANGEVIEW LIBRARY DISTRICT

FIRST GRAPHICS | BODY SYSTEMS

A Tour of Your Muscular and Skeletal Systems

by Katie Clark

illustrated by Chris B. Jones

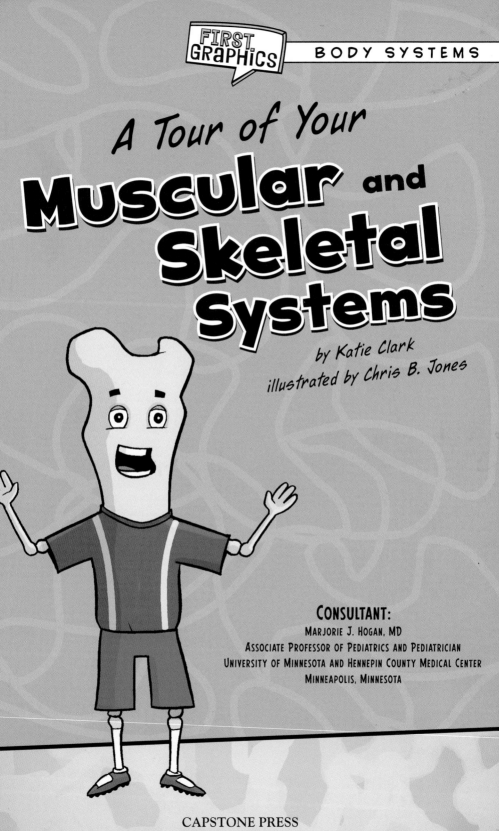

CONSULTANT:

Marjorie J. Hogan, MD

Associate Professor of Pediatrics and Pediatrician

University of Minnesota and Hennepin County Medical Center

Minneapolis, Minnesota

CAPSTONE PRESS

a capstone imprint

First Graphics are published by Capstone Press,
1710 Roe Crest Drive, North Mankato, Minnesota 56003.
www.capstonepub.com

Copyright © 2013 by Capstone Press, a Capstone imprint.
All rights reserved.
No part of this publication may be reproduced in whole or in part, or
stored in a retrieval system, or transmitted in any form or by any means,
electronic, mechanical, photocopying, recording, or otherwise, without
written permission of the publisher.
For information regarding permission, write to Capstone Press,
1710 Roe Crest Drive, North Mankato, Minnesota 56003.

Library of Congress Cataloging-in-Publication Data
Clark, Katie, 1962–
  A tour of your muscular and skeletal systems / by Katie Clark ; illustrated by
Chris B. Jones.
     p. cm.—(First graphics. Body systems)
  Summary: "In graphic novel format, follows Bradley Bone as he travels through
and explains the workings of the human muscular and skeletal systems"—
Provided by publisher.
  Includes bibliographical references and index.
  ISBN 978-1-4296-8605-1 (library binding)
  ISBN 978-1-4296-9326-4 (paperback)
  ISBN 978-1-62065-263-3 (ebook PDF)
  1. Musculoskeletal system—Juvenile literature. I. Jones, Chris B., ill. II. Title.

QM100.C53 2013   2011051827
612.7—dc23

Editor: Christopher L. Harbo
Designer: Lori Bye
Art Director: Nathan Gassman
Production Specialist: Kathy McColley

Printed in the United States of America in Stevens Point, Wisconsin.
032012   006678WZF12

Table of Contents

Going for the Goal 4

Bones and Muscles 6

Working Together 14

Keep Kicking 20

Glossary 22
Read More 23
Internet Sites 23
Index 24

Going for the Goal

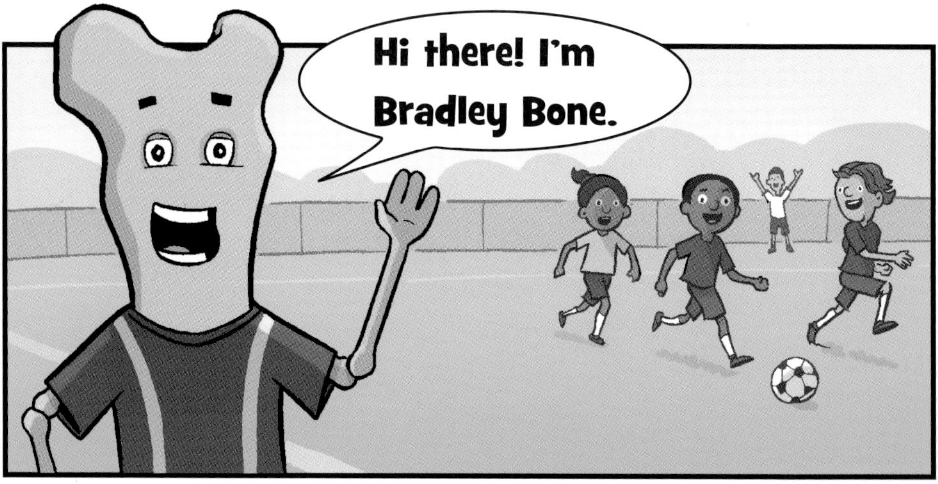
Hi there! I'm Bradley Bone.

You're just in time for the big game.
Join me as I help Kenny kick a goal!

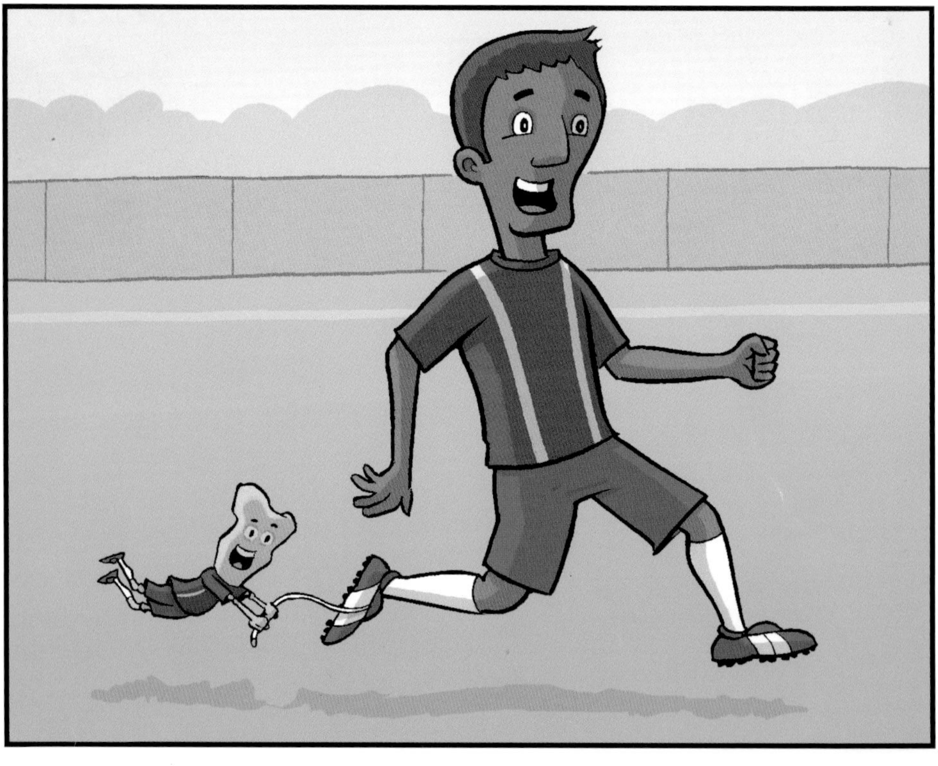

To run and kick, Kenny uses his muscular and skeletal systems.

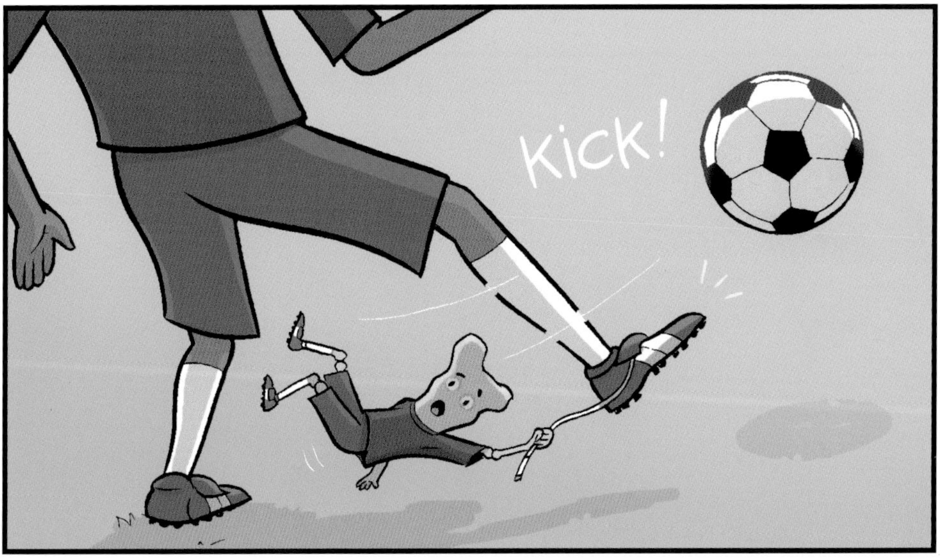
KICK!

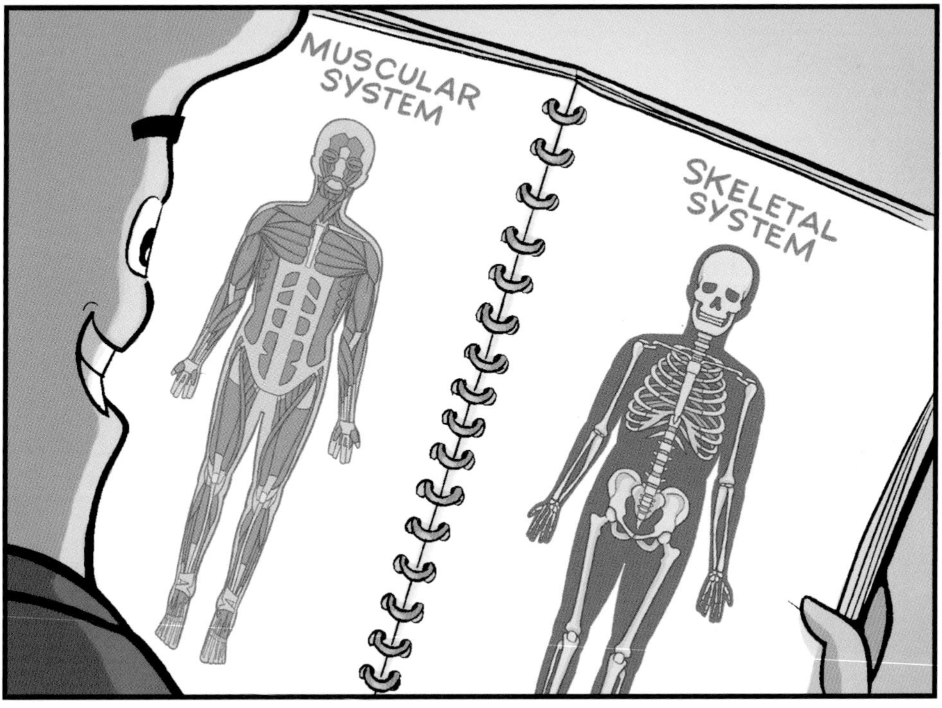
MUSCULAR SYSTEM
SKELETAL SYSTEM

These systems are made of muscles and bones.

Bones and Muscles

Your body has more than 200 bones.

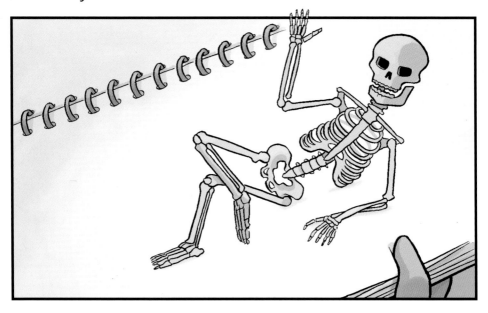

Each of these bones has three layers.

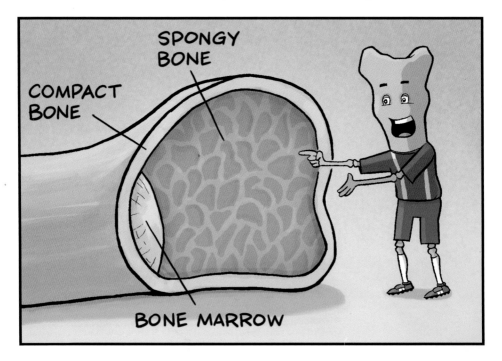

SPONGY BONE

COMPACT BONE

BONE MARROW

The outside layer is hard, like a shell.
This shell makes bones strong.

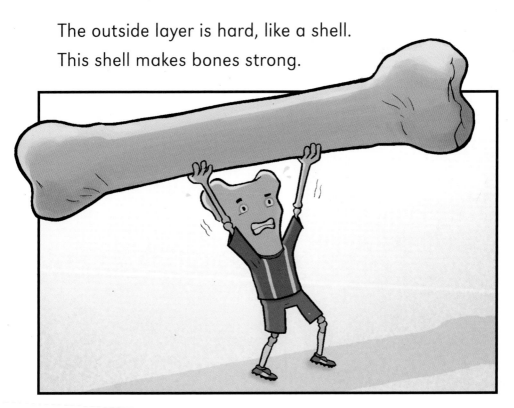

The inside layers are soft, like a sponge. These layers
make blood. They also store water and minerals.

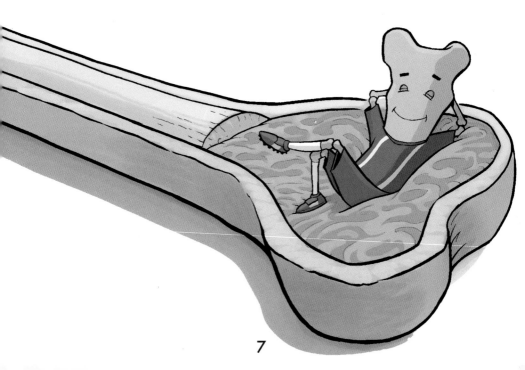

Bones hold you up and give your body shape.

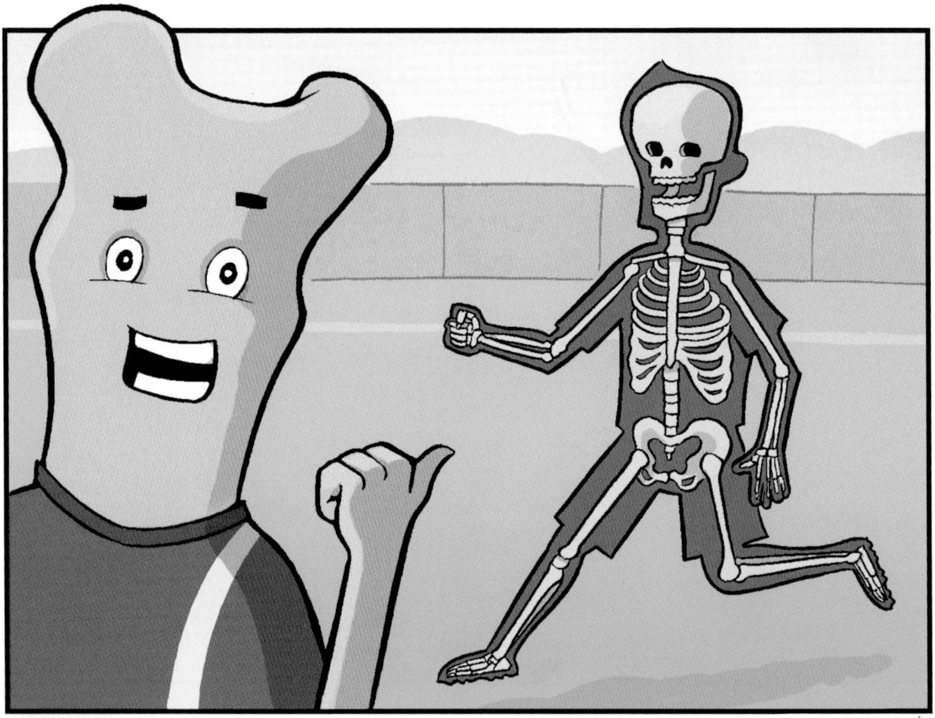

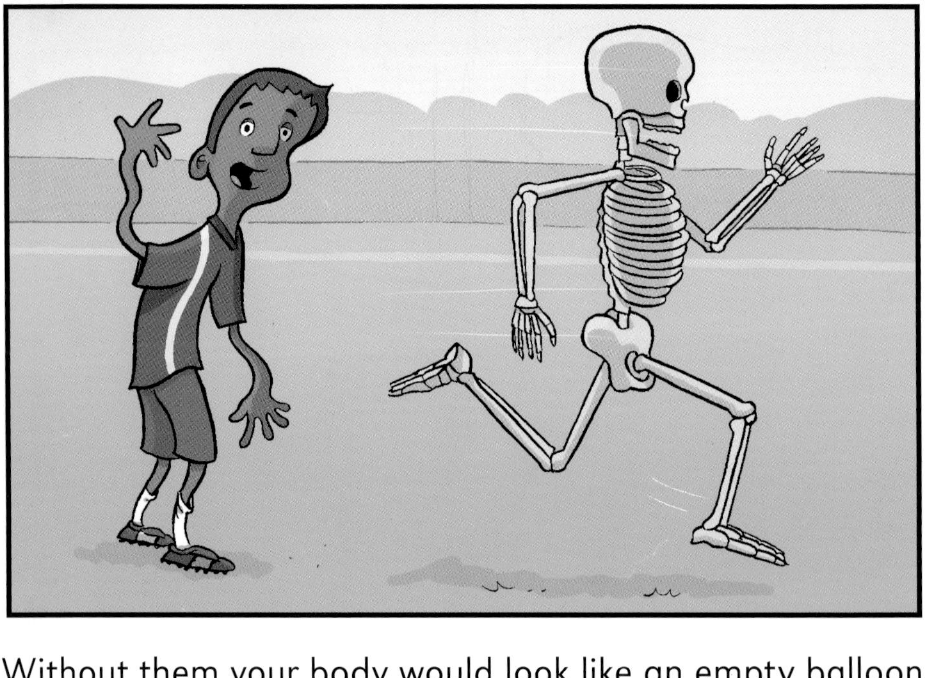

Without them your body would look like an empty balloon.

Bones also keep you safe.

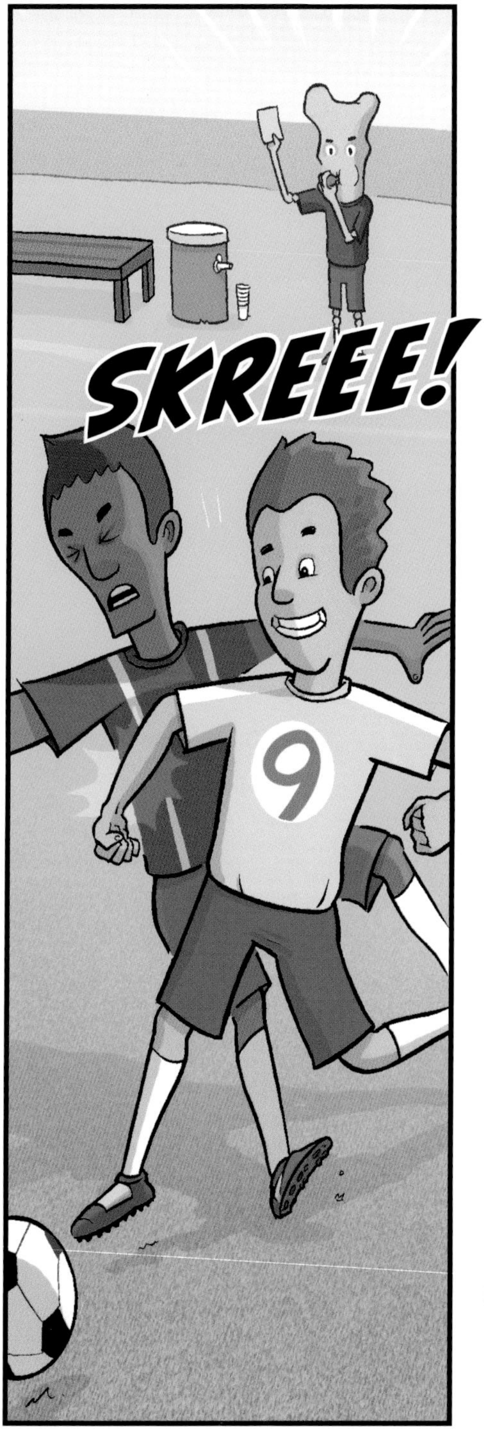
SKREEE!

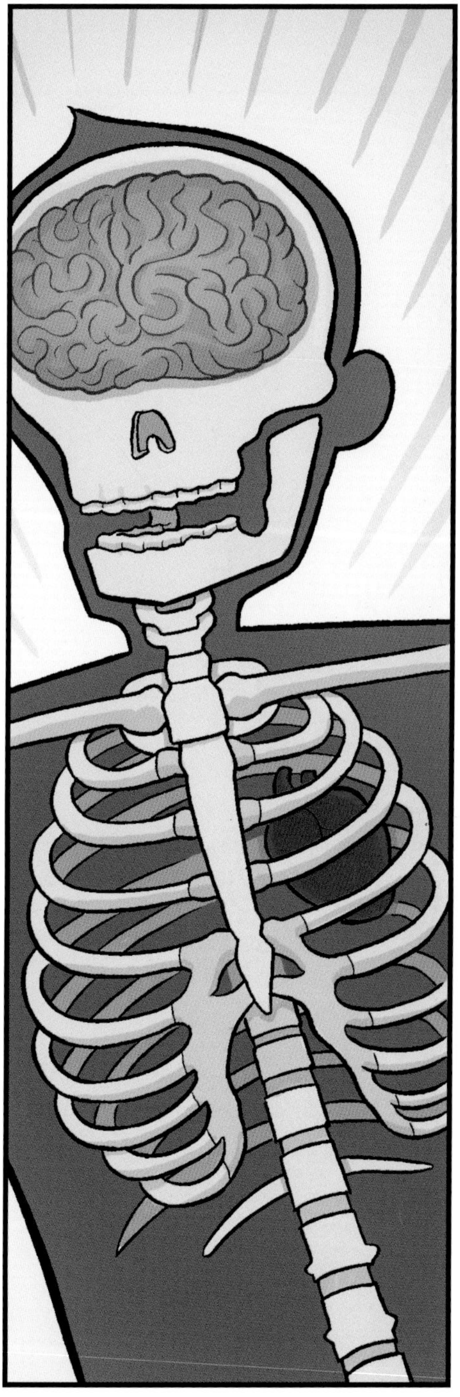

They protect organs such as your brain and heart.

Muscles connect to the bones in your body.

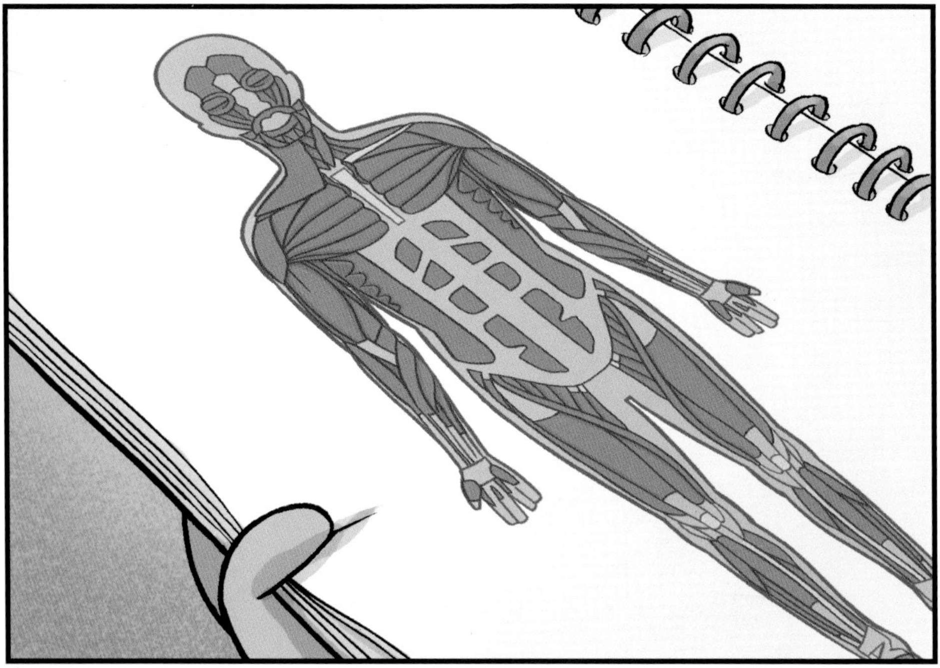

More than 600 muscles cover your bones from head to toe.

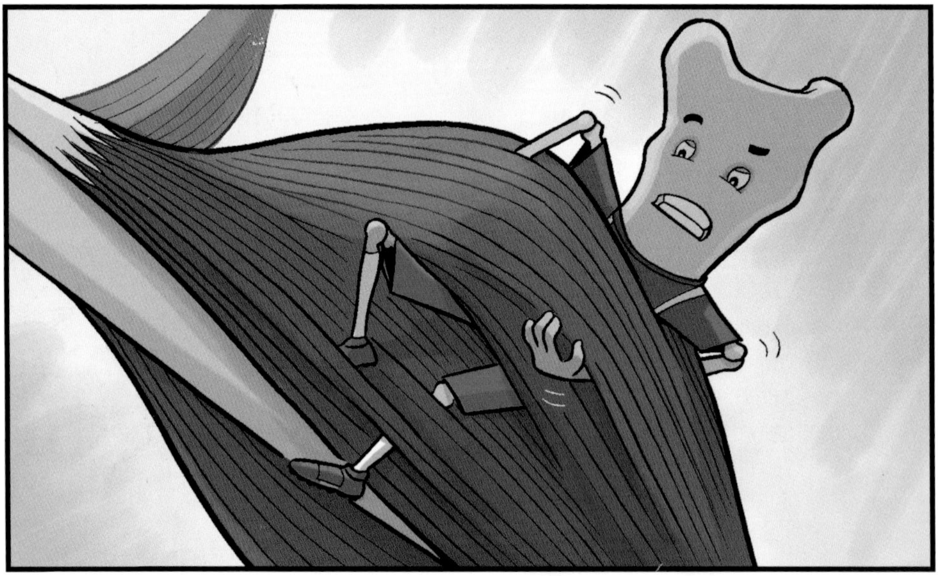

Many of these muscles look like thick rope.

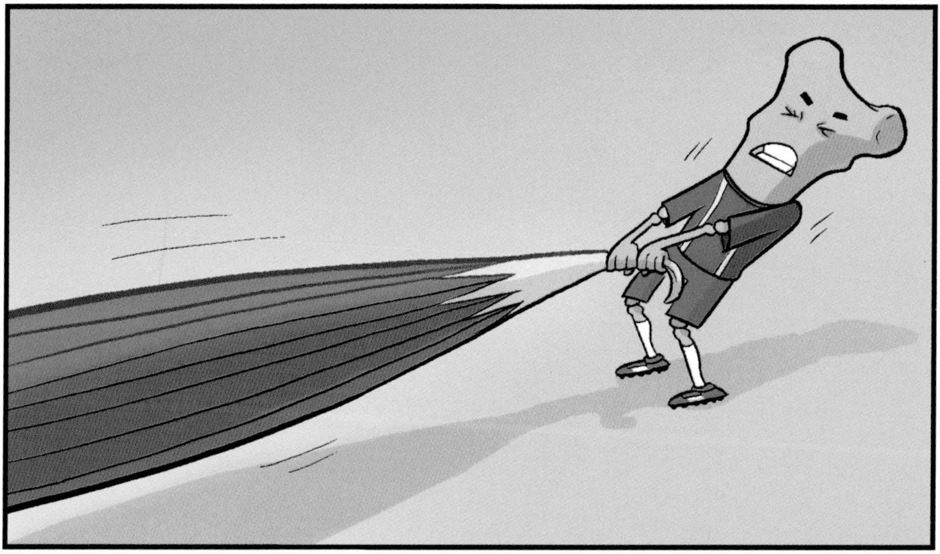

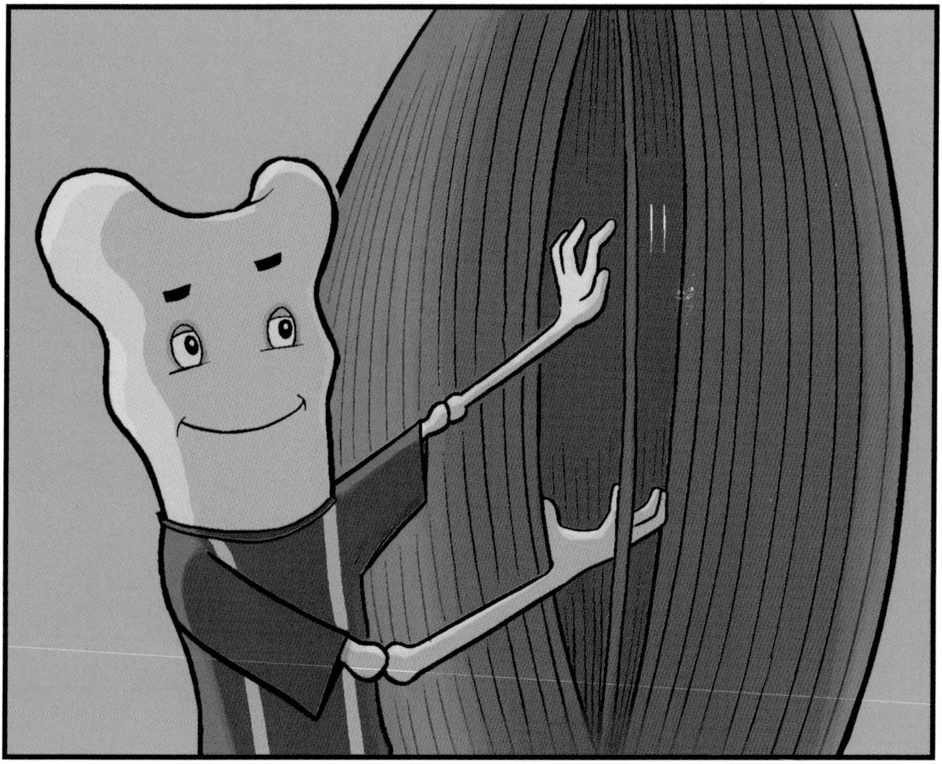

They have fibers to make them strong.

To kick a soccer ball, your muscles team up.

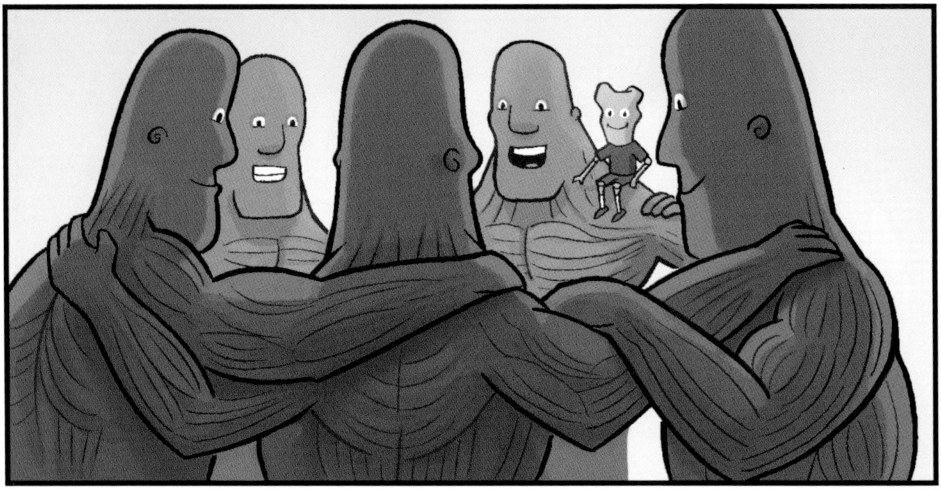

One muscle pulls your leg back.

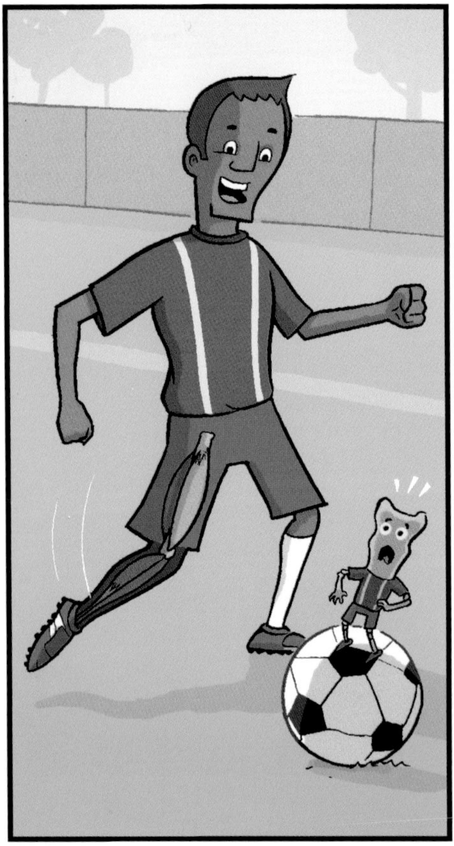

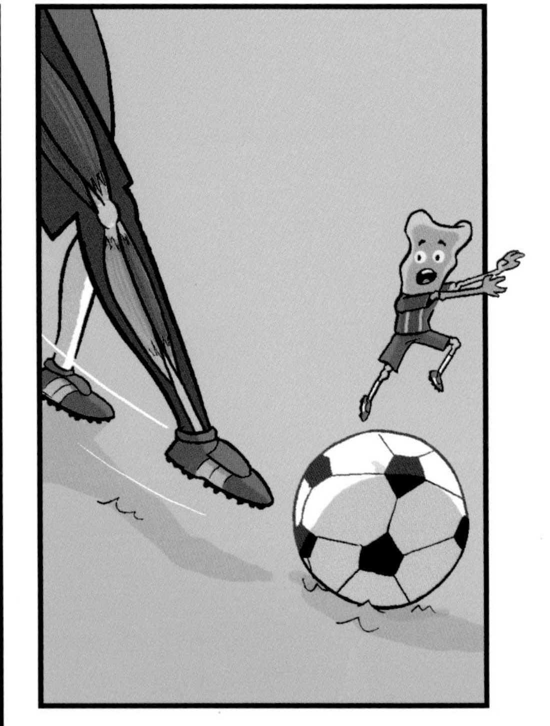

Another muscle pulls it forward.

Your muscles and bones send the ball flying!

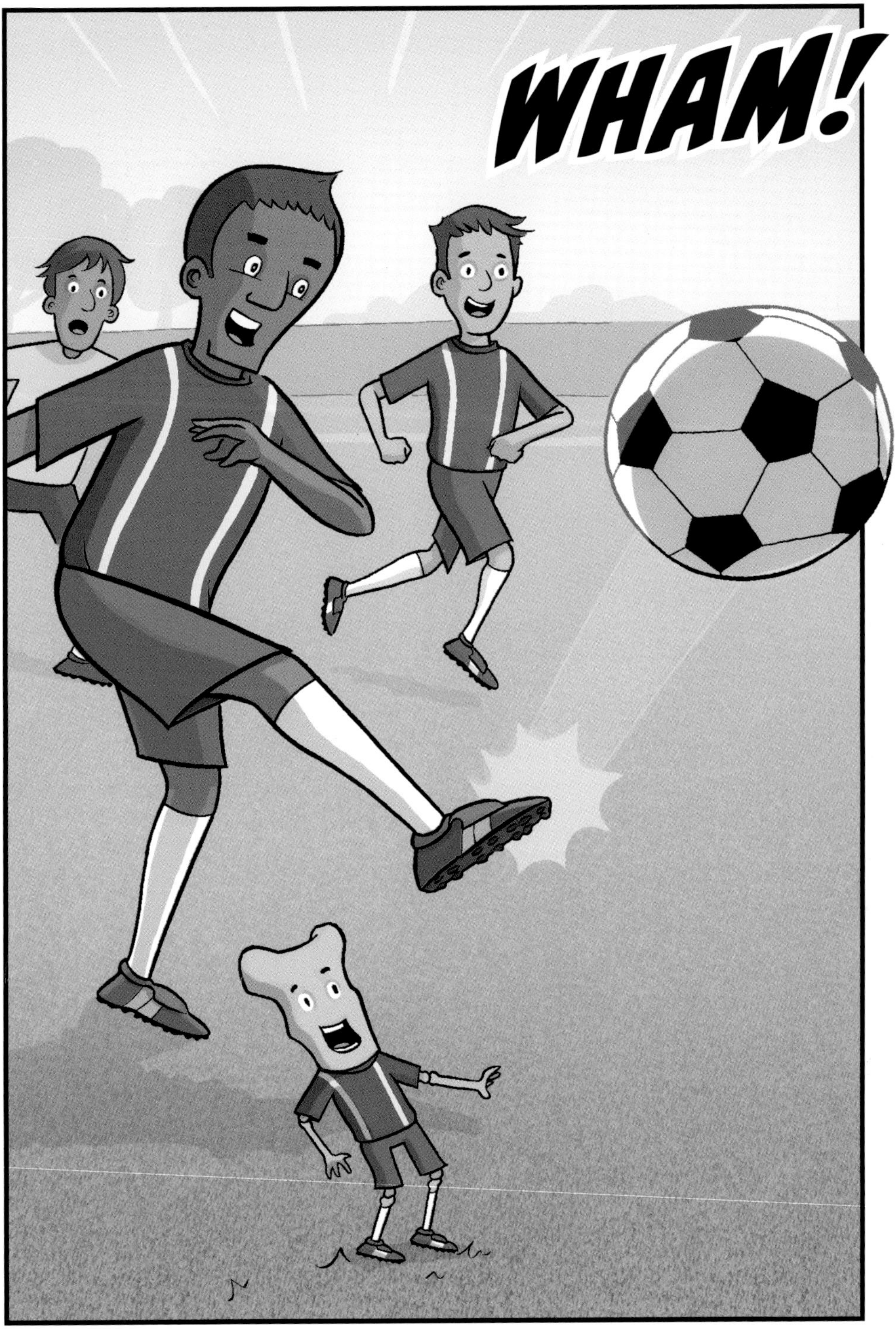
WHAM!

Working Together

Muscles and bones use joints, ligaments, and tendons to help you move.

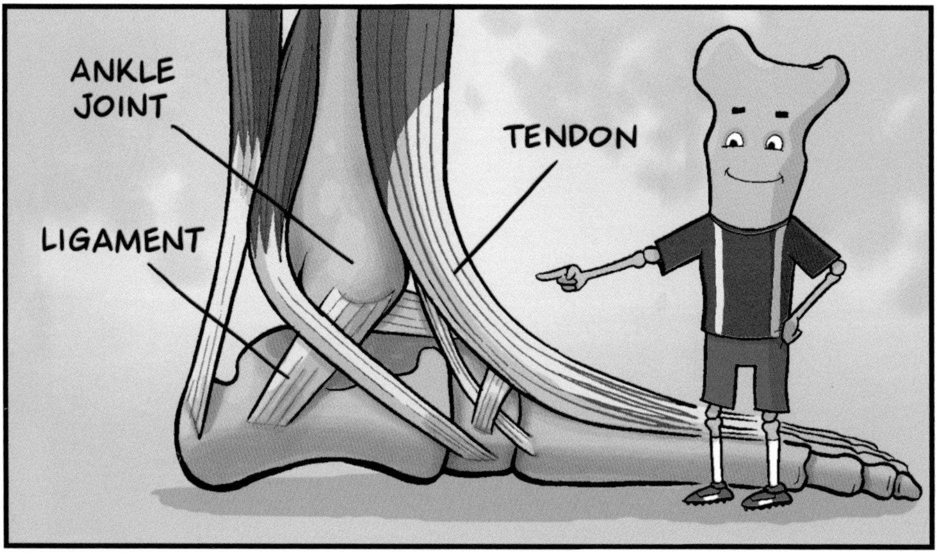
ANKLE JOINT
TENDON
LIGAMENT

Bones come together at joints.

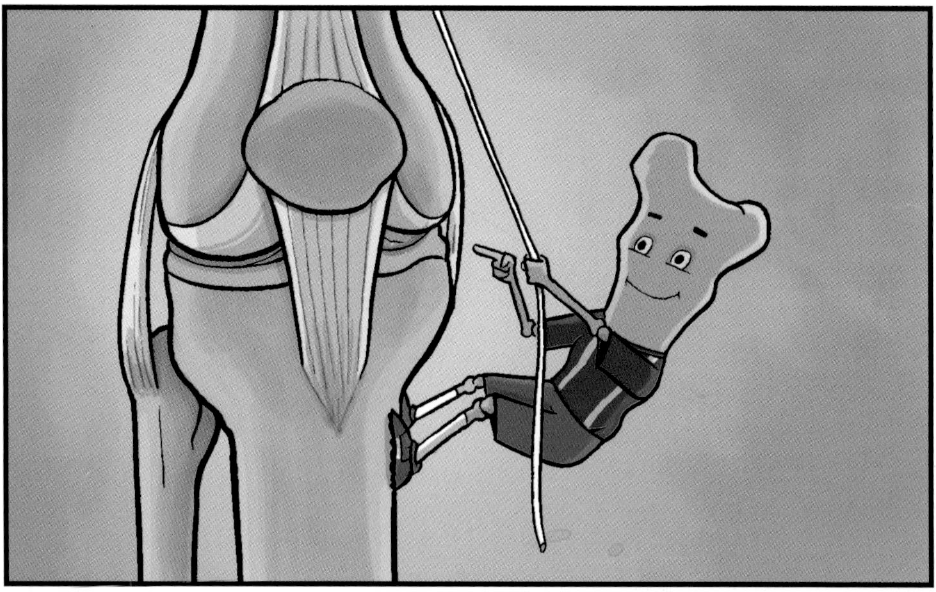

Some joints move like a joystick.

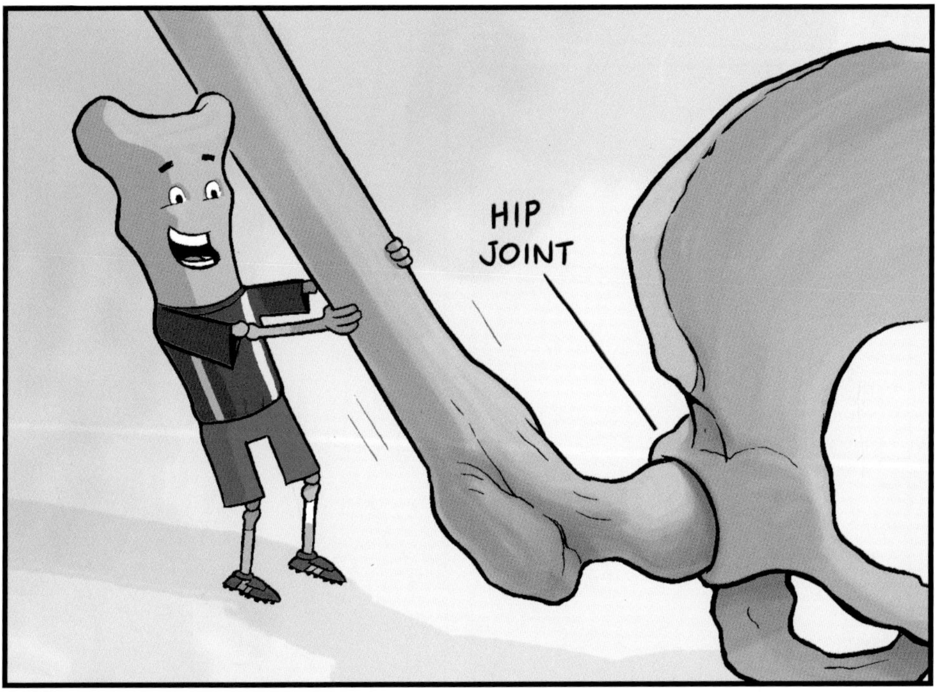
HIP
JOINT

Other joints open and close like a door.

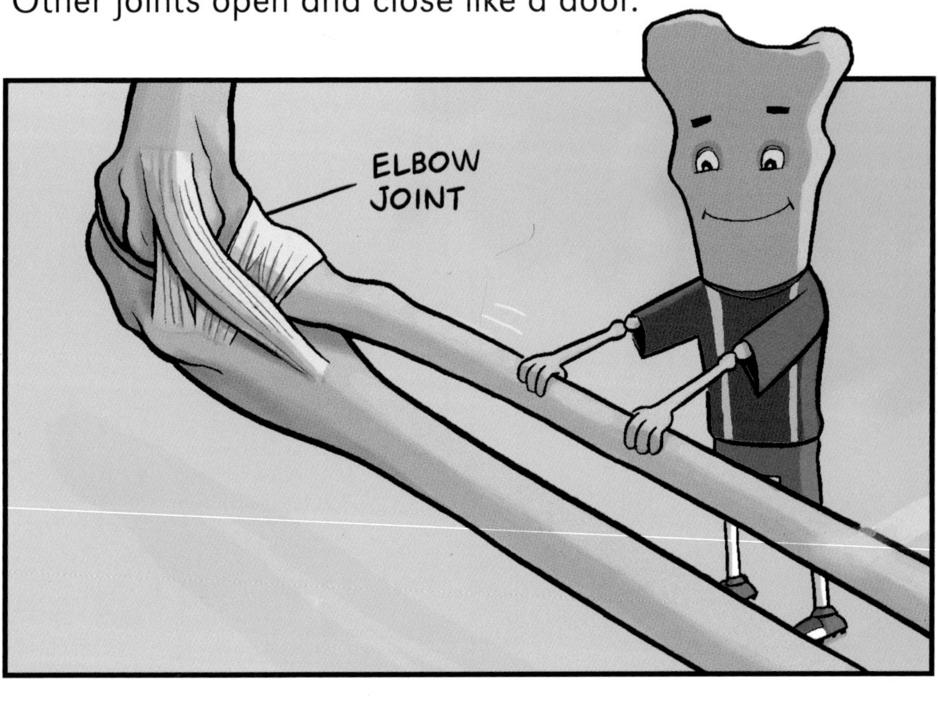
ELBOW
JOINT

Ligaments connect bones at the joint.

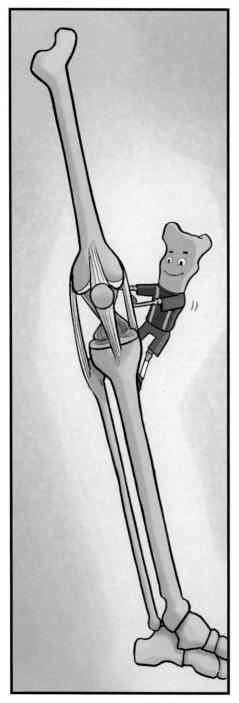

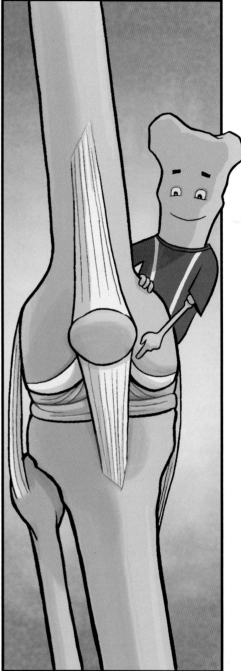

They keep bones in place.

Ligaments also control which way a joint moves.

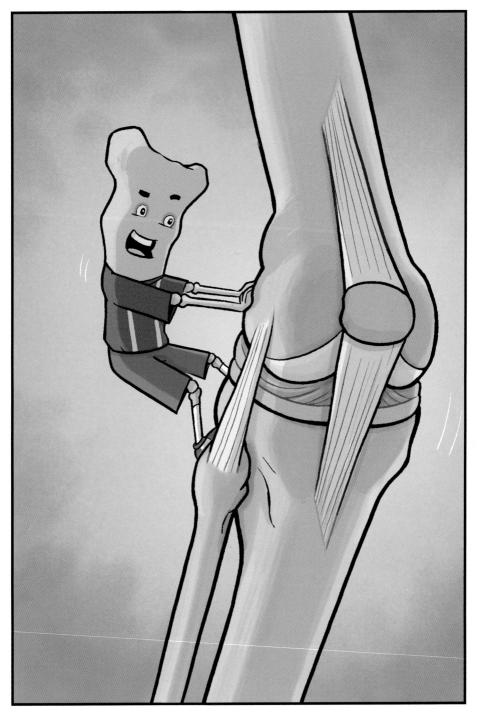

They stop joints from bending the wrong way.

Tendons connect muscles to bones.

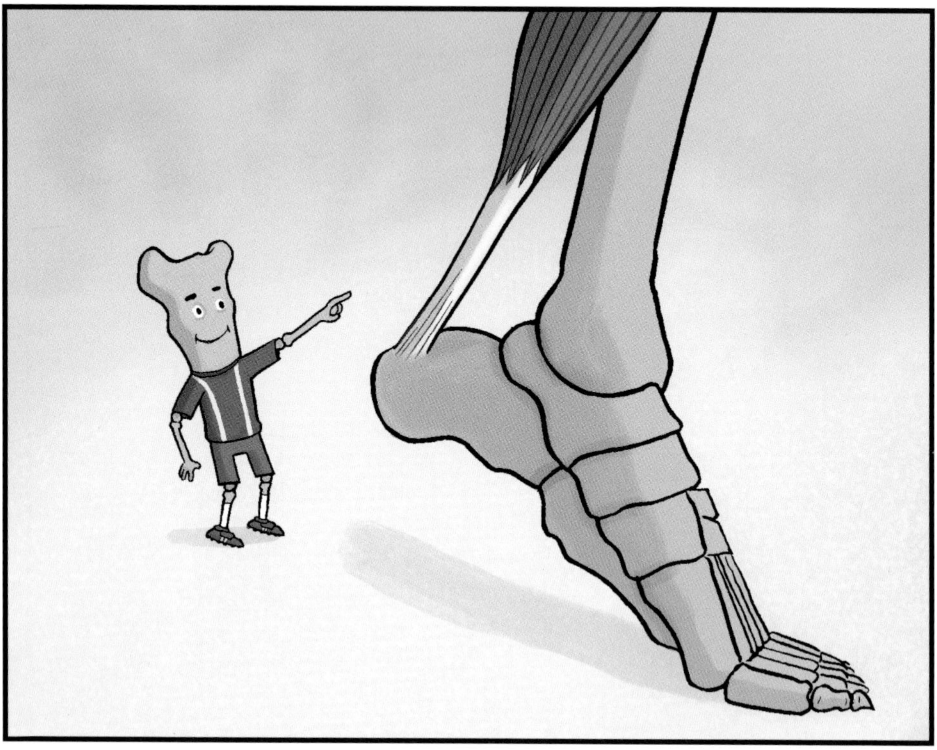

Tendons are stretchy like a rubber band.

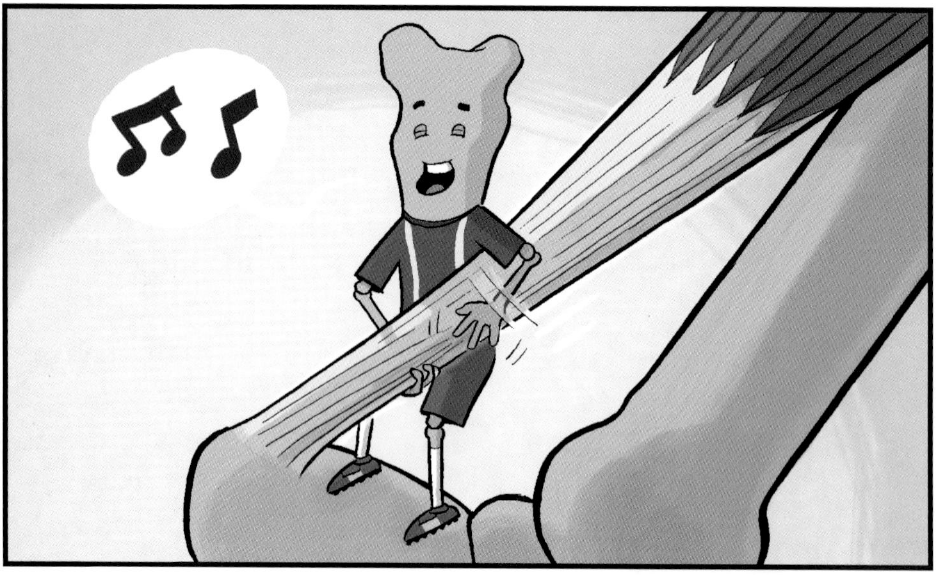

When a muscle tightens, it tugs on the tendon. The tendon pulls the bone.

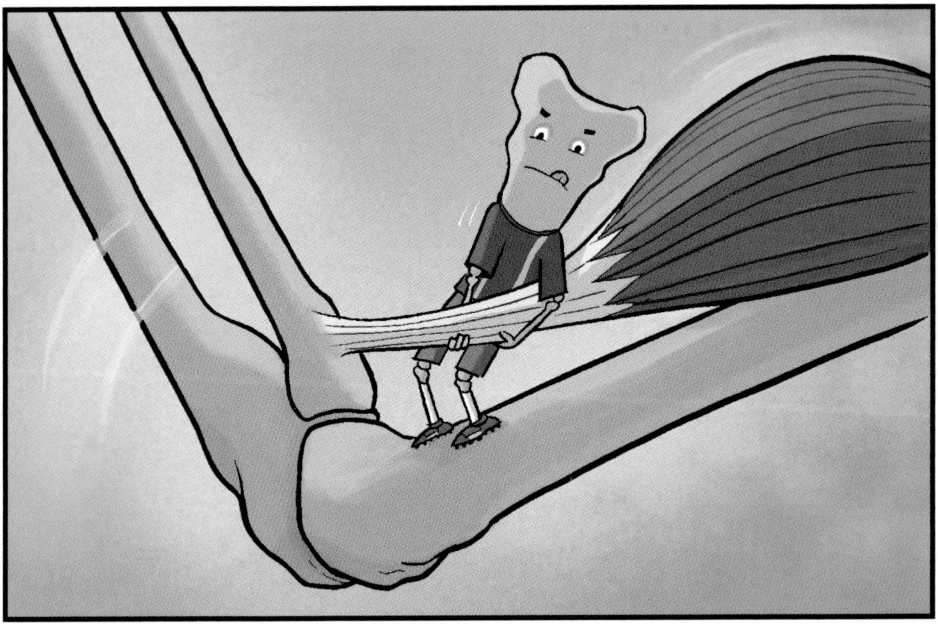

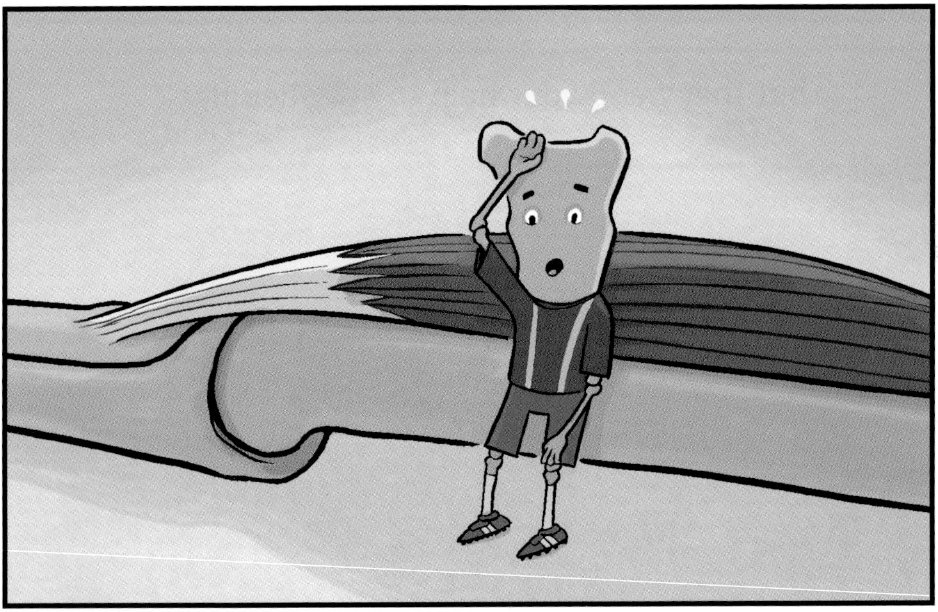

When the muscle relaxes, the tendon stops pulling. The bone moves back to where it started.

Glossary

fiber—a long, thin thread of material

joint—the place where two bones meet; knees, elbows, hips, and shoulders are joints

ligament—a band of tissue that connects or supports bones and joints

mineral—a substance found in nature that is not an animal or a plant; calcium is an important mineral for bones

organ—a part of the body that does a certain job; your heart, lungs, and kidneys are organs

tendon—a strong band of tissue that attaches muscles to bones

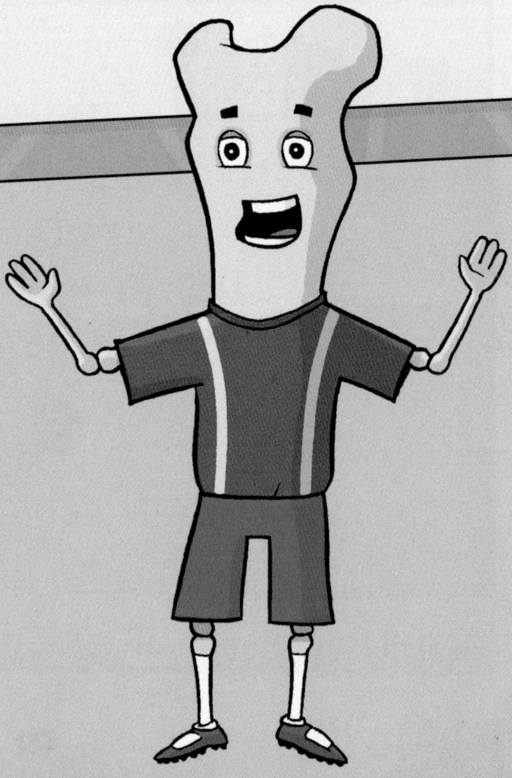

Ballard, Carol. *How Your Body Moves.* Your Body at Work. New York: Gareth Stevens Pub., 2011.

Burstein, John. *The Mighty Muscular and Skeletal Systems: How Do My Bones and Muscles Work?* Slim Goodbody's Body Buddies. New York: Crabtree Pub., 2009.

Johnson, Rebecca L. *Your Muscular System.* How Does Your Body Work? Minneapolis: Lerner Publications Company, 2013.

Jordan, Apple. *My Bones and Muscles.* My Body. New York: Marshall Cavendish Benchmark, 2012.

Internet Sites

FactHound offers a safe, fun way to find Internet sites related to this book. All of the sites on FactHound have been researched by our staff.

Here's all you do:

Visit *www.facthound.com*

Type in this code: 9781429686051

 Check out projects, games and lots more at
www.capstonekids.com

Index

blood, 7

bones
    layers of, 6–7
    number of, 6
    purpose of,
       8–9, 20

exercise, 21

food, 21

joints, 14–15,
    16, 17

kicking, 4–5,
    12–13, 21

ligaments, 14, 16–17

minerals, 7

muscles
    number of, 10
    purpose of, 10, 20

organs, 9

staying healthy, 20–21

tendons, 14, 18–19

water, 7

Titles in this set:

A Tour of Your
Circulatory System

A Tour of Your
Digestive System

A Tour of Your
Muscular and Skeletal Systems

A Tour of Your
Nervous System

A Tour of Your
Respiratory System

FIRST GRAPHICS